Just Real Useable
TAROT SPREADS

Anne-Marie Bond

Just Real Useable
TAROT SPREADS

Enhance your existing tarot skills and achieve spot on readings, using
60 amazing, everyday life tarot spreads!

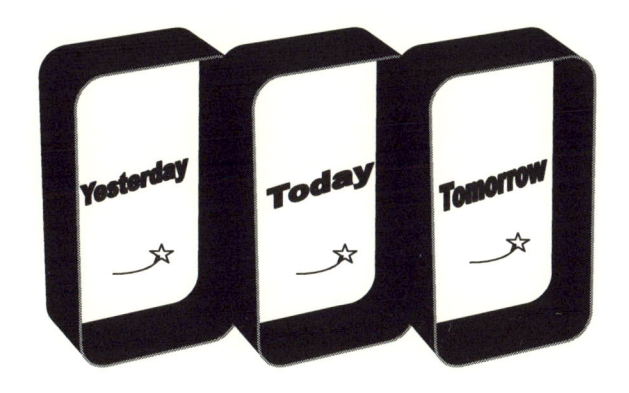

Suitable for: Novices: Intermediates: Advanced

By Anne-Marie Bond

©SpiritualStars

Anne-Marie Bond

SpiritualStars
First published 2012

© Copyright Anne-Marie Bond 2012

Anne-Marie Bond asserts the moral right to be identified as the author of this work

All rights reserved. No part of this book may be reproduced, stored in an information storage and retrieval system, or transmitted in any form or by any means, electronic, mechanical, photocopying, recording or otherwise, without the prior permission of the publisher. Nor is it to be otherwise circulated in any form or binding or cover other than which it is published.

You are not permitted to change title headings or amend any written layout meanings, please keep the layouts and their meanings as shown.

Published ©Spiritualstars
ISBN 978-1-4709-7328-5

Did you like this book?
Please contact the author by email:

spiritualstars@gmail.com

DEDICATED TO:

The Divine Spirit

To my spirit guides: Marcus and Dali and to my spiritual family & friends. Thank you for your patience, your understanding, your love and continuous guidance, without you, this book would never have materialised.

To my Mum and Dad for their advice, guidance and support but most of all for their unconditional love that allowed me to be the person I am.

To all those that walked alone, lost and isolated, feeling different from the rest, but through Tarot have learnt to understand themselves that little bit more, enabling them to realise their own truth and calling in this world.

Finally, to my spiritual stars circle of friends and students....

Long Live Spiritualism!

Anne-Marie Bond

OTHER BOOKS BY THE AUTHOR:

My Lifetime Journal by mum   ISBN 978-1-4461-8637-4
A book every mum should give their child

CONTENTS PAGE

Forward by Anne Jirsch .... Page 9
List of Tarot Spreads .... Pages 11-13
List of Sample Spreads .... Page 14

Authors greeting .... Page 15
Using this book .... Page 17
Introduction to Tarot .... Page 19
Majors verses Minors .... Page 20
How to use the cards .... Page 21
Daily practice advice .... Page 22
Reading tarot for yourself .... Page 23
Sample daily tarot card reading .... Page 24
Reading tarot for others .... Pages 25-28

Different preparation shuffling and cutting methods .... Page 29
Tarot spreads .... Pages 31-81
Sample spreads .... Pages 83-91

Workshops / My Services .... Page 93
Contact Me .... Page 94

Anne-Marie Bond

FORWARD
By Anne Jirsch

I have been working with tarot for over thirty years and I can honestly say the cards never fail to amaze me. Their accuracy and insight can be life changing, helping people through difficult times in their lives and guiding them to a better life.

Over the years I have noticed how many people who love tarot have a huge pile of books on the subject and many different packs. I've been teaching tarot for a long time and most information on the subject is complicated and confused.

Anne-Marie's book is different. It shows you easy, step by step spreads that anyone can use and the range of subjects will cover anything you need to know. If you read cards or intend to, keep this one book by your side and you will have access to all the information that you need. It is not a book to read quickly and toss aside more a tool to refer to.

In future when I teach tarot I will advise my trainees to buy a copy of Anne-Marie's book.

Anne Jirsch

Anne-Marie Bond

Just Real Useable TAROT SPREADS

Choose Your Reading: Tarot Spreads - Love / Romance

General Love Relationship Spread ....Page 32

I'm in a relationship – Where is it heading? ....Page 33

I'm in a relationship – It's complicated, do I stay or go? ....Page 33

I'm in a relationship – Me, my partner and 'that' other person.................................Page 34

I'm in a relationship – Will they commit one day? ....Page 35

I'm in a relationship – Will I have children? ....Page 35

I'm in a relationship – Why is my partner becoming distant towards me? ....Page 36

I'm in a relationship – Are we going to separate / divorce? ....Page 37

I'm in a relationship – The good, the bad and the unexpected...............................Page 37

I'm single – My future lover, when, where and how? ....Page 38

I'm single – In the last 3 months I've split from my ex, will we re-unite? ....Page 39

I'm single – I've seen someone I fancy, do they fancy me too? ....Page 39

I'm single – Out of the blue, my ex has just contacted me, why? ....Page 40

I'm single – Why can't I meet anyone compatible and will I someday? ....Page 40

I'm single – Will I have my own family one day (marriage / children)? ....Page 41

I'm single – Recently, I've been thinking about my ex, why? ....Page 41

I've just met someone (dating) – Date 1 went really well, are they the one? ....Page 42

I've just met someone (dating) – I feel something is being kept from me ....Page 43

I'm dating two people – Which one is better for me? ....Page 43

I've just met someone (dating) – We are meeting for our first date, any tips? ....Page 44

I'm in two intimate relationships – Should I stay with this one or that one? ....Page 45

I'm kind of in a relationship – I still see my ex, but they are also seeing someone else (A)Pages 46-47

I was in a relationship – We had a massive row & I think I've messed it up, have I? (A) ....Page 48

11

Choose Your Reading: Tarot Spreads - Work / Career / Projects

I'm in work – What does the future hold? ....Page 51

I'm in work – What should I be wary of / or look forward to? ....Page 51

I'm in work – Should I look for another job or will things improve? ....Page 52

I'm in work – I've been asked to attend a meeting, will my role be affected? ....Page 52

I am self-employed – How does my 'mobile' business look over the next 6 months? ....Page 53

I am self-employed – What should I know about my business partner? ....Page 53

I am self-employed – Why is my business failing? ....Page 54

I am going to become self-employed – Will my new business become successful? ....Page 55

I have my own business/company – What can I do to gain more customers/clients? .....Page 56

I have my own business/company – The good, the bad and the unexpected ....Page 56

I am not working – Will I find a job soon? ....Page 57

New Job – I have an interview coming up, any hints or tips? ....Page 57

I am working on my new business project – Will I complete it and will it be successful? ...Page 58

Choose Your Reading: Tarot Spreads – Finances

My finances – Are dire, why and will they improve? ....Page 59

My finances – Will my idea, my business plan, be financially successful? ....Page 60

My finances – Will I be mega rich? ....Page 61

My finances – I lent some money out, will I get it back? ....Page 61

My finances – The good, the bad, the unexpected ....Page 62

My finances – The reason why I'm broke and struggling financially ....Page 62

Choose Your Reading: Tarot Spreads – General Miscellaneous

My yesterday's, my today's and my tomorrow's ....Page 64
Generally, what does the next 3 - 6 months look like for me? ....Page 65
I'm thinking of starting / continuing my diet plan, will I lose weight? ....Page 66
I will be travelling soon, the good, the bad and the unexpected...........................Page 67
What are my biggest obstacles right now, known and <u>unknown</u> to me?............................Page 67

How can I achieve a higher spiritual awareness? ....Page 68
I'm told I'm psychic – am I and should I develop it? ....Page 69
What is the best option for me – this choice <u>or</u> that choice? ....Page 70
I've been picked to go on a dinner / date / cooking / TV show, any tips?........................Page 70
Our department is going for a re-shuffle, will I be affected? ....Page 71

I've got an idea to write a book/script would it be successful? ....Page 71
My friend is going through a hard time, what can I do to help? ....Page 72
All about me: Me, myself and I..Page 72
In the future, will I achieve my main desire, my dream, and my goals? ....Page 73
Sometimes I feel lost, isolated, depressed and that my life is going no-where ....Page 73
Yes, No, Maybe (Single question answers) ....Page 74
12 months future possibilities reading ....Page 75

Tarot Spreads: Bonus Anne-Marie's General Readings for Advanced Readers

20 mins - Specific spread for any area (A) ....Page 78
25 mins - Past Life spread – who was I (A)...Page 79
25 mins - Future Life spread – who will I be (A)..Page 80
45 mins - Future Life Progression spread within the next 5 years (A) ....Page 81

List of Sample Spreads

My yesterday's, my today's and my tomorrow's ....Page 85

New Job – I have an interview coming up, any hints or tips? ....Page 86

I am self-employed – How does my business look over the next 6 months? ....Page 87

All about me: Me, myself and I ....Page 88

Yes, No, Maybe (Single question answers) ....Page 89

I'm single – Why can't I meet anyone compatible and will I someday? ....Page 90-91

Authors Greeting

Welcome to my book. I'm Anne-Marie Bond, a psychic medium, tarot reader, advanced weight-loss consultant, teacher, author, crystal healer and qualified *FLP + PLR practitioner. I created this book due to the number of requests I have received over the years by students and clients who wanted real-life tarot spreads to help improve their own <u>existing</u> tarot reading skills.

I have been reading tarot for over 25 years and to people from all over the globe, varying from private sittings, to email or telephone readings and now with new technology via Skype. I have also completed readings by post (before computers were widely available to the general public). I **<u>live</u>** to help other people in any way I can, especially to help expand their knowledge, build their confidence & self-value.

I receive great feedback from my clients, students and friends that I read for, whether it's because I have helped them to lose weight, improve their relationship status, start a new career or just in general to help them evolve to a <u>higher</u> spiritual level of awareness. Teaching tarot to various people over the years has given me a huge amount of pleasure, especially teaching those wishing to read tarot for others at a professional level, either privately from home or working on the psychic tarot phone lines, or even at psychic events. Never forget, as I tell all my tarot students: As a reader your <u>main aim</u> should be that upon completion of reading for a client, friend, or the Joe public, your recipient leaves the session feeling empowered, motivated, hopeful and happy! Receiving feedback is just an additional bonus.

I really hope that you enjoy working with my spreads as I have many times over, hence the title of the book:

Just Real Useable TAROT SPREADS

*FLP Future Life Progression - PLR Past Life Regression

Anne-Marie Bond

Using this book

You will find that the majority of spreads inside this book have been titled using 'certain questions or phrases' that I have personally created over the years solely upon the questions asked repeatedly by various clients. This book may not be suitable for absolute complete beginners because it does not teach the 'meanings' of the tarot cards but simply how to lay them out in preparation for a reading.

As a *novice (little experience) or as an intermediate or advanced user I'm sure you'll find many spreads useful and helpful to you, not only for your own personal benefit but for your recipients too. Simply turn to any spread on any page and have fun! Perhaps try some of the spreads on yourself first and then try them out on others, you'll have hours of fun and you will be so amazed with the accuracy they produce!

I would recommend as a polite suggestion however, that if you are a novice, perhaps familiarize yourself with the more BASIC and INTERMEDIATE level spreads first, before, attempting the more advanced ones... (Indicated with an **A**) *Just a suggestion!*

The spreads are designed to bring peace of mind through clarity and understanding of your situations that could enable you to make better choices and decisions. You will notice I have not included any 'health' related or 'legal issues' spreads because unless you are a doctor or lawyer it's best to avoid reading these areas for others. If a particular spread position relays to a 3rd person's point of view and how they feel or what's going on in their life, these should only be viewed as a possibility and not as a definite.

***Novice: Some understanding of the importance of the Major & Minor arcana is required including a basic understanding of each card within a normal standard 78 tarot deck. A bonus would be that that novice has previously read for friends or family on occasion and is now ready to expand their reading knowledge on a deeper level.*

Anne-Marie Bond

Introduction to Tarot

As a novice, intermediate or advanced tarot reader, I already expect that you will have some basic understanding of Tarot and its purpose, i.e. to be used as a psychic tool to look at the recipients past, present and possible future situations. Some psychic's believe however that the tarot cards should not to be used to fortune-tell, whilst the opinions of other psychics will differ. I see the cards as a way to look at the present circumstances to locate the obstacles and thus find advice / guidance from the cards in order for the recipient to overcome them or gain clarity at least.

Looking into the future is a form of prediction no matter what anyone says... (my opinion) but, and it's a big BUT, as the reader when providing a 'future' tarot reading be sure to let your recipient know that your interpretation of the message & outcome of the cards, cannot come with any <u>guarantees</u>. This is simply because each recipient has their own free-will to make any choices or decisions that they see fit, regardless of the advice/guidance given by the cards. By gaining clarity from the tarot cards simply allows the recipient to see a snippet of the possibilities that could lay ahead based upon on the decisions they are thinking of making, or have already made.

Tarot cards should only be used to gain advice and guidance; however, although at times they may indicate a timing span, they should not be used or relied upon as a specific <u>timing</u> tool. There will be times when the recipient(s) are not meant to know, 'the when', or even 'the how' in some cases, therefore allow the cards to unfold as they should. Never try to force the answer and avoid asking the same question over again, especially on the same day.

In my opinion, each tarot card has the possibility to contain 25 or more different meanings. You don't have to learn them all, but as a budding tarot reader and possibly with an intention to read at a professional level, it's vital that you learn how to build a relationship with your cards and most importantly learn how to read on an intuitive level, this will divide you from being an **OK book,** tarot reader to an **amazing, gifted, intuitive** and <u>recommended</u> one!

Good Luck x Anne-Marie x

Majors verses Minors

A normal standard Tarot deck consists of 78 cards.

22 Major arcana cards (major situations in the recipient's life – normally beyond their control) and **56 Minor arcana** cards (minor situations that the recipient can usually control depending on their choices/decisions). The word – Arcana - is a Latin word which means 'big secret', therefore the 22 Major cards will help you to find out the 'Major Secrets' and they carry more weight in a reading than the 56 Minor arcana, although the Minor arcana shouldn't be undervalued as they provide the more intimate details behind the scenes.

The Major arcana represents the most important aspects of your life, your major feelings, your major life changes, endings and beginnings for example getting married or going through a divorce. The heavier presence of the major cards in a reading, suggests the possibility of something 'major' about to take place in your life. Some of the major cards i.e. like the **Death** or **Tower** cards will represent the changes in your life that you have no control of, so by understanding the purpose of the cards will eliminate the surprise element and allow you to be prepared both mentally and psychically for the 'changes' that are about to take place.

Some professional psychics prefer to use only the 22 Major arcana when reading for clients, family or friends. I prefer to use all 78, and sometimes I may even use 2 decks!

How to use the cards

Conducting a reading by following a tarot spread (layout) ensures that a structure is in place throughout the reading. It also allows the recipient to understand and follow the route and path of the reading. Advanced tarot readers will also benefit from using the spreads within this book, or at times may prefer to use their own 'free-flow' style (randomly turning cards over without a structure). Sometimes this can work really well because then you are not tied down to specifics of that particular position and definition; however this works best when you have obtained good experience at reading the cards for yourself and others (successfully).

When conducting my readings I intuitively decide whether I will use the free flow method or a specific spread according to the area chosen by my client.

Treat your cards kindly, they will help to not only, provide the answers you need for yourself but for your recipients too! Use your own preferred shuffling and cutting method and stick with it.

Each tarot card contains various amounts of images / symbols and pictures and as a reader it will help your interpretation that little bit more if you understand them, but it is **not essential** for you to learn them all because when reading for yourself or others you do not need to interpret every symbol on each tarot card. You will usually see just one or two aspects of the card and then your intuition takes over. Once you have given your interpretation, move on to the next card. Just look at the images and go with your first gut reaction, follow your intuition and usually you will be right!

Finally, summarize all cards in order to polish off the reading for your recipient!

Daily practice advice

The difference <u>between</u> an amazing intuitive tarot reader and an OK run of the mill one, in my opinion, is the person who has learnt to read tarot for them-selves. Some psychics may comment that it's impossible to read for your-self, but as I read for myself all the time, **so can you**!

Lots of continued practice will make you a better, stronger and more capable psychic tarot reader. Once you begin reading for the public, you have a responsibility and duty to do the very best you can for their highest good. Your reading should be conducted with the highest intention of love, honesty and integrity, especially if you have to relay an answer that the recipient was not expecting to hear. Please bear in mind, if the answer is a No, find out why and end the reading on a positive note!

Learn how to read tarot for yourself

EXERCISE:

1. Within an hour of waking, shuffle your cards, cut, take the top card and look at it.
2. In a journal write down your 1st thoughts/impressions of how you feel your day <u>may</u> progress.
3. Before bed, look at what you wrote and compare your days' activity to see how accurate you were.
4. Doing this on a daily basis especially for the first 3 months of learning tarot will strengthen your intuitive connection to the cards!
5. When you feel confident you should increase your daily card routine to 2 cards.

Practicing daily no matter your <u>level</u> of expertise
will ensure you build a stronger bond with your cards.

Reading tarot for yourself

Q: Why wouldn't a professional tarot reader want to read tarot for themselves?

A: Just because 'one' maybe a professional psychic tarot reader doesn't automatically mean they wouldn't share life's ups and downs and at times make the wrong choice/decision. That person may have found them-self at a crossroads or perhaps they are so emotionally involved they are unable to see the situation from an objective point of view and may need a different prospectus on their situation!

As long as you can interpret the cards from an objective point of view and overcome your personal emotions/attachment to the situation then you should have no problem reading for your-self. Feeling confident about the outcome will take time.

Even though I have the capability of reading for my-self, at times I may find myself too emotionally attached to a situation and therefore at those times I may obtain another psychic's perspective on the situation. I find the best method to read for yourself (in my opinion) is to complete the daily tarot reading exercise (shown on the previous page) until you have reached a good success rate, then upgrade to more cards.

NOTE:
It's very rare that a tarot reader will get 100% correct on every reading they conduct as they are simply the 'interpreter' and as such may interpret the message with its full meaning at times. However, no matter your level, there is always something to learn in each reading you do.

When you feel comfortable with the daily One Card routine, try an upgrade and conduct a more in-depth spread (reading) on yourself.

Novice Progression

STEP 1 - Daily 1 card routine: 3 months practice is good then upgrade to 2 cards	**1 to 2 cards**
STEP 2 - Use a past, present and future general (all areas) spread on yourself	**3 cards**
STEP 3 - Use an all about me: Me, Myself and I spread	**8 cards**
STEP 4 - Specific area spread	**13 cards**

SAMPLE OF A ONE CARD - DAILY TAROT READING:

MONEY

ACE of COINS

©Spiritualstars

Example of what you may write in your daily journal

Today: I may receive money – gain a gift – or have an opportunity presented to me to raise my income. New business ideas comes to mind and perhaps discussed with another person, or someone gives me their idea or perception on how I can make more money. Possibility of making initial plans to travel.

Reading tarot for others

Taking on the responsibility of reading for others should be solely to help those people discover answers, gain clarity and peace of mind. Don't decide to become a tarot reader simply for money otherwise you will find your tarot reading journey to be a short one. The universe will know your inner intention and therefore please ensure you embark on this journey for the highest good of others and yourself.

Over the next few pages, I have listed 22 points that may help you to gain a deeper understanding the role a tarot reader plays when reading for other people. These are just 'my personal suggestions' and you use whatever feels right for you.

THE TAROT READER

1. It is not your role to inform someone of an impending death.

2. If you are asked a question that results in a NO (which the recipient really didn't expect to hear), it's your duty to be honest and give the answer in an empathic way. Please end your readings on a positive note, so if the answer is a NO, look into it and find out why the NO came about, and what positives the recipient can take from it.

3. Your role is to provide advice & guidance in answer to the recipient's question. Never give your personal opinion but just the advice of the cards; otherwise your recipient won't understand if the advice is coming from you as your opinion or that of the cards.

4. Never allow your emotions to run riot. If you see something sad, or get so deep into the recipients emotions (if they are crying) you must suck it up! As the reader you cannot give a reading if you are over emotional and crying also. It's ok to emphasise with the recipient, but you must remain professional at all times, after all, that's why they are seeking your service.

5. You will not be able to read for every single person that requests a reading from you. For whatever reason (usually beyond your understanding) you may find that the reading just isn't working. If that happens, be honest with the recipient and let them know that you are not finding the energy three-way link between yourself the cards and the recipient, strong enough to conduct the reading.

6. Be honest, never fabricate and never turn the outcome of a reading into something you want the recipient to hear!

7. Be kind with your words, be clear (don't ramble or mumble) and don't be afraid to ask the recipient a question about their circumstances in order to help you ascertain what the cards are trying to say. Example: If you ask the recipient which area they wish to look at and they say **"LOVE"**, it is perfectly fine for you to ask them if they are they in a relationship or not. This will help you provide more definition in that area, but of course, the other alternative is to free-flow without asking any questions.

8. Be positive, upbeat and truthful. No matter what, never apologise as long as you are doing your best and reading with integrity then <u>stand</u> by what you see. By saying "you're not sure" leaves the recipient wondering if there was anything else in the reading you were not sure about and their faith in you may decrease rapidly!

9. If you find that your recipient appears to be too over emotional it's ok to ask if they would like to cancel or postpone the reading.

10. When asked a question that could result in an answer the recipient **may not** want to hear, ask them if they are prepared emotionally and mentally for the answer no matter which way it unfolds. This usually gives the recipient time to re-think and work out if in actual fact, they are actually mentally and really **prepared** for the 'truth'.

11. Paying or non paying recipients deserve your same respect, understanding and 100% of your focus. You are only the messenger; the cards provide the answers through their advice and guidance.

12. Never be judgemental, no matter the circumstances of the recipient (i.e. involved with more than one relationship at the same time), it's your responsibility to be honest and with a non-judgemental point of view.

13. Be nice, pleasant and welcoming to the recipient as they will be nervous and could be coming to you for the first time. First impressions count and if you want them to come again, be FRIENDLY, but not overbearing either, don't argue, shout or be condescending to your recipient. Don't over stare at the recipient and make them feel conscious, they have feelings and are coming to you for **guidance**.

14. Ensure your reading area is clean, quiet and inviting. Remember you want them to come again and to tell others. Looking professional & ensuring that you look hygienic sets off a great 1st impression.

15. If you feel tired or unwell or not 100% on the day of the reading, cancel it. The recipient will respect you more for wanting to reschedule the appointment, to ensure they get the very best out of you.

16. If your recipient is being unresponsive to your questions, being rude, aggressive or acting at all in a manner you deem as inappropriate, feel free to ask them if something is wrong and would they prefer you to stop the reading or continue?

17. Do not allow yourself to be bullied by the recipient, if they refuse to accept your interpretation then allow it to be so. As long as you remain calm, collected and at all times professional (never raise your voice or use inappropriate language) inform the recipient politely that it's your interpretation and of course they have the 'free-will' to believe the cards or not as you are only relaying what you see.

18. Try not to use many different spreads on the same client within the same reading session. Choose a general one that you feel comfortable working with and then perhaps use a specific spread or fee-flow for YES or NO questions. Keep to a format that works best for you and that you feel comfortable with. Slowly introduce new spreads when you feel ready to experiment and remember each reading will be different from the last. Even as an advanced tarot reader you will never stop learning from the cards. Record your new meanings into a journal!

19. If a recipient asks you a question and you really don't know the answer, BE HONEST and let them know that you don't know because it could be that the cards have chosen <u>not to answer</u> for the recipients own purpose. It may be that the recipient is not supposed to know the answer at that particular time for whatever the reason and if it's not working, don't force it and always be honest!

20. If a recipient at the start of the reading says **"Oh I know you won't be able to read for me, no-one ever can"**. As the reader, you should <u>stop</u> the reading immediately and reply to the recipient **"You are right"**. Rustle up your cards and let the recipient know that you are unable to continue or conduct the reading.

    When asked **"Why?"** simply reply **"Because you told me I wouldn't be able to read for you"**. I can assure you that they **would not** say that again to another psychic! *Remember, you are not reading to be tested; you are reading to genuinely help people with genuine issues.*

    Now this may seem a harsh response... however, I am saving you from future misery, because once you have invested your time and effort into that recipient, their response at the end will usually be **"I told you so, I told you that you wouldn't be able to read for me"**. They will then totally disregard your reading and some with some recipients you may decide to sit there longer trying to persuade the recipient that you <u>can</u> read for them. Before long, many hours may have passed and once the recipient has drained you completely, will then **say "oh that was very good, yes I understood everything"**. By then you will have no energy and will be left with your mouth opened wide. *We call these type of recipients... Psychic vampires... they want to suck every last drop of energy you have.*

21. Act confident and be confident in any reading you conduct, because you are only the messenger. Trust in your own abilities because you are AMAZING!

22. Before each reading send a little prayer to the spiritual world asking for their love and support in order to help and assist you to relay accurate answers to your recipient. Don't forget to thank the spirit world and the universe for their help after each reading. After all, that's where the guidance truly comes from!

I hope you found some of these points helpful!

Different Preparation Shuffling and Cutting Methods

Before choosing a tarot spread (unless indicated differently), please don't forget to shuffle and cut your cards using any of the methods demonstrated <u>below</u> but, if you have your own preferred method, please feel free to use it.

I generally use **step 1** for all the readings I conduct for myself, clients, friends and family. Also I may at times turn over an additional card as the emphasis card especially if the last card appears to be negative as I always believe where there is a negative, a positive must follow! Readings should always end on a **positive note**, and as the reader although you can explain to the recipient the good and bad points of the negative card, it's ok for you to draw another card to see how things improve. You decide!

Preparing Your Cards Before Using A Tarot Spread

At the start of any reading you conduct always have the question or area in mind <u>before</u> shuffling. I avoid engaging in a conversation with the client about other matters whilst shuffling. Confuse the cards and you'll get a confused response!

With the area or question in mind…. choose any shuffling, cutting method below

1) Shuffle your deck > cut into 2 piles on a hard surface> put the bottom pile on top of the first making one stack > take the desired number of cards from the top

2) Shuffle your deck > cut into 3 piles on a hard surface > randomly re-order each pile on top of each other creating one stack > take the desired number of cards from the top

3) Shuffle your deck > cut into 2 or 3 piles > randomly choose ONE pile to work with>take the desired number of cards from the top

4) Shuffle your deck > (no cutting) > Take desired number of cards from the top

5) Shuffle your deck > fan them out (faced down) onto a table > randomly select the desired number of cards for that spread

Good luck and have fun!

Anne-Marie Bond

TAROT SPREADS

Love - Relationships

GENERAL 'LOVE' RELATIONSHIP SPREAD

1) Your current circumstances/feelings regarding relationships
2) Your mental attitude towards relationships
3) How you feel regarding your existing or non-existent relationship situation
4) How your relationships have been in the past
5) What you like in a partner
6) What you dislike in a partner
7) What you generally bring into a relationship (positive or negative)
8) What <u>you</u> could change in order to improve your relationship situation
9) What type of partner would suit you best
10) What kind of relationship you like / brings out the best in you
11) Your relationship (whether current or new) will be like in the future
12) Where your focus should be at present in general

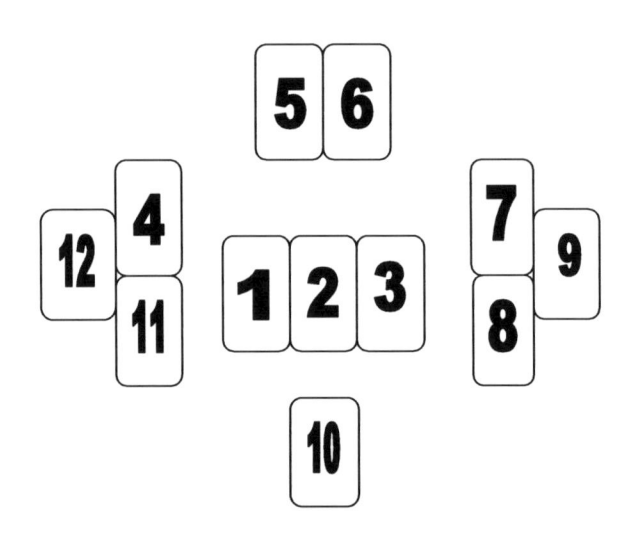

I'm in a relationship – Where is it heading?

1) The Past: How the relationship was
2) The Present: How the relationship appears to be now
3) The Future: How the relationship could develop

I'm in a relationship - It's complicated, do I stay or go?

1) The energy of the relationship (good/bad)
2) How you feel about the relationship
3) How 'the other person' may feel about the relationship
4) The obstacle / problem
5) If you go.... the next six months for you
6) If you stay... the next six months for you

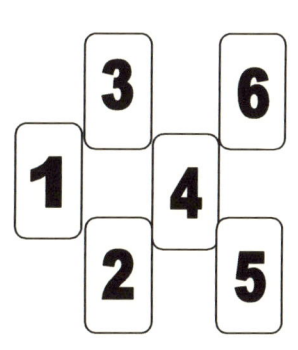

I'm in a relationship – Can I trust my partner?

1) Your personality / character / your focus
2) Your partners personality / character / their focus
3) The current energy of the relationship
4) Your partner's possible views on the relationship right now
5) Your partner's current feelings towards you
6) Your partner's hopes / desires for the direction of this relationship
7) Changes/developments to your relationship over the next few weeks
8) Can you trust your partner
9) Does your partner feel that they can trust you
10) Likely outcome of 'your' relationship over next 10 months

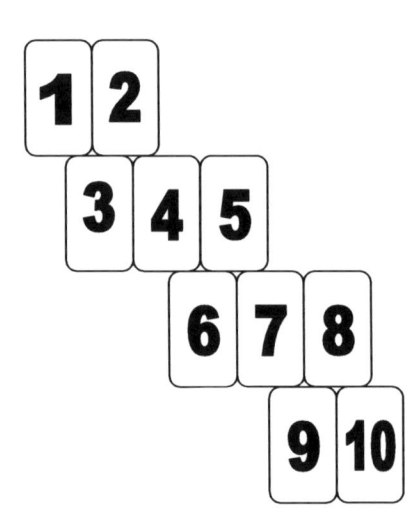

I'm in a relationship – Will they commit to marriage one day?

1) The current energy of the relationship
2) How your partner may view the relationship at present
3) Your views on the relationship
4) What your partner may want from the relationship <u>short</u> term
5) What they may want from the relationship <u>long</u> term
6) Why they appear <u>not to be</u> committing to the relationship right now
7) Likelihood of marriage together in the future (near)
8) Likelihood of marriage together in the future (far)

I'm in a relationship – Will I have children?

1) What's great about the relationship currently
2) Changes / developments over the next 5 months
3) How children would enhance your relationship
4) How your partner may feel about having children
5) Likely outcome of seeing children in <u>your</u> near future

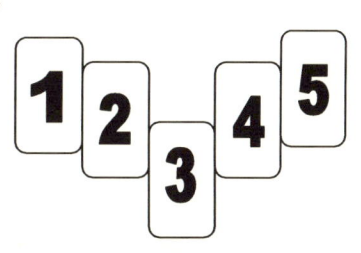

I'm in a relationship – Why is my partner becoming distant towards me?

1) The current energy of the relationship
2) Relationship Obstacles / Problems
3) How you could possibly overcome this obstacle
4) How your partner may feels towards you presently
5) Their current focus (in general)
6) What they like/love about you
7) What they dislike/loath about you
8) What they like/love about themselves
9) What they dislike/loath about themselves
10) Possibility of why they could be becoming more distant towards you
11) Advice / guidance for you, now is the time to:
12) Advice / guidance for you, now is not the time to:

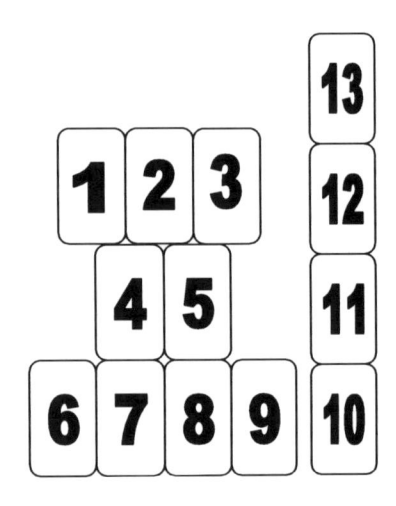

I'm in a relationship – Are we going to separate / divorce?

1) Current energy of the relationship
2) The relationships possible obstacles / problems
3) How your partner may feel towards the relationship
4) Your partners possible hopes/dreams for the relationship
5) How you may feel if a separation happens
6) How your partner may feel if a separation happens
7) Possibility of a separation / divorce in the near future
8) The relationship 8 months from now

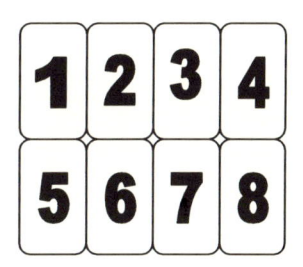

I'm in a relationship – The good, the bad, and the unexpected

1) Current energy of the relationship / the direction its taking
2) The good points about the relationship
3) The bad points about the relationship
4) The unexpected - over the next 4weeks/months expect......

I'm single – My future lover, when, where and how?

1) Your mental or emotional state in regards to relationships
2) Your 'ideal' person (personality / characteristics / ethics)
3) Likelihood of a relationship for you within the near future
4) Your next love (r) (personality / characteristics / ethics)
5) Their 1st impression of you
6) Your 1st impression of them
7) All about the meeting, when, where and how
8) What you can do to be ready for this new love
9) Will it be short term or long term (decide this by turning over another 2 cards…)

Any page, knight or king cards in either position indication of short or long term

No court card could indicate **'only time will tell'** as the recipients answer

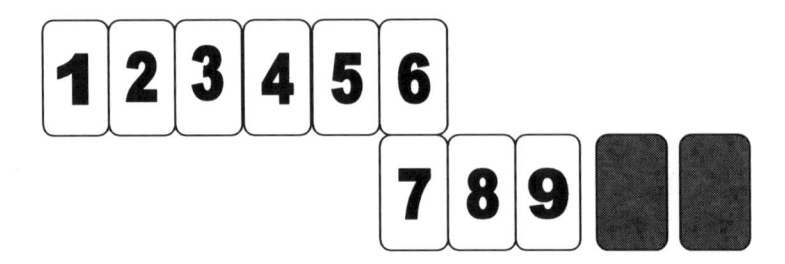

I'm single – In the last 3 months I've split from my ex, will we re-unite?

1) Your current situation (in general)
2) Their possible current situation (in general)
3) What made the relationship good for you
4) What made the relationship good for them
5) How you currently feel towards your ex
6) How your ex could possibly feel towards you presently
7) Energy surrounding the split
8) What is likely to hinder/stop a re-union
9) Likelihood of a re-kindled romance sometime in the future

I'm single – I've seen someone I fancy, do they fancy me?

1) Why your energy is attracted to the other person
2) The possibility of the other person feeling attracted to you
3) Where their focus could be right now (in general)
4) Their possible view/feelings towards relationships (in general)
5) What they may like in a partner
6) What they may dislike in a partner
7) The possibility of a connection between you both developing

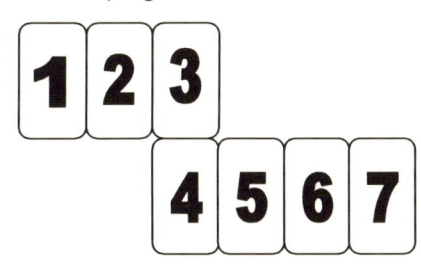

I'm single – Out of the blue, my ex has just contacted me, why?

1) The past energy between you and your ex
2) Energy surrounding their current situation
3) Their possible reasons/motives for getting in touch with you
4) How things 'may' progress between you both in the future

I'm single – Why can't I meet anyone compatible and will I someday?

1) Your current mental / emotional state
2) Your past relationships
3) The positives you bring into a relationship
4) The type of person that would be compatible to you
5) What hinders you currently attracting a decent partner
6) What / Who could help you find someone compatible
7) All about the type of person you will probably meet next
8) Possible timings / and how or where the meeting takes place
9) <u>Generally:</u> what is coming up for you soon   *(card 9 placed in the centre)*

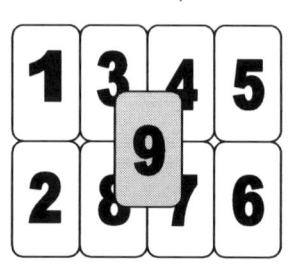

I'm single – Will I have my own family one day?

1) Your current situation in general
2) Past relationships that may still affect you in some way
3) Where your focus should be right now
4) Possibility of you being in a significant relationship over the few years
5) Possibility of marriage for you over the next few years
6) Possibility of children over the next few years

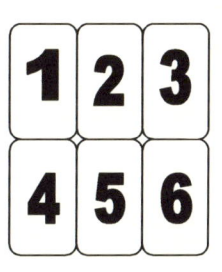

I'm single – Recently I've been thinking about my ex, why?

1) Energy behind the relationship breakdown
2) How you currently feeling towards your ex
3) How your ex may currently feel towards you
4) Why you have been thinking about them
5) Possibility of who / what they are currently thinking about
6) The energy of a likely re-union between you both
7) If you did re-unite, how would it progress

I've just met someone (dating) – Date 1 went really well, are they the one?

1) The current energy of the dating relationship between you both
2) What you like/love about them
3) What they may like/love about you
4) What you may still need to learn about them
5) What they may still need to learn about you
6) What's good about your 'union' so far
7) How you could enhance their world
8) How they could enhance your world
9) Prospects of an intimate relationship developing between you both
10) What should be your next move
11) What their next move is likely to be
12) What development can you expect over the weeks/months
13) Surprise for you in this 'area' 13 days / weeks / months

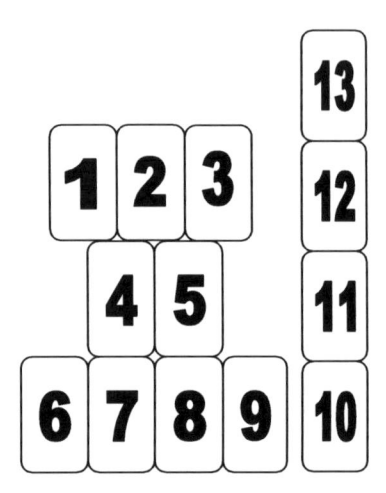

I've just met someone (dating) – I feel something is being kept from me

1) The current energy of the dating relationship between you both
2) You're concerned because... (the root of your concern)
3) The direction the relationship could go if you let your concerns go
4) How they may feel about you / direction of the dating relationship
5) What they might be keeping from you (their current focus)
6) Your current dating relationship progress's to…….

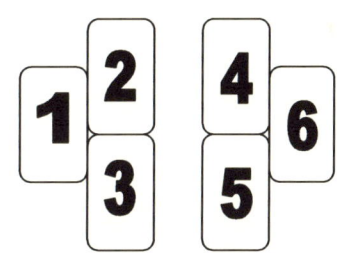

I'm (dating) two people – Which one is better for me?

1) How you see person 1
2) How you see person 2
3) Relationship 1 person how they may see you
4) Relationship 2 person how they may see you
5) Possible short term with person 1
6) Possible short term with person 2
7) Possible long term with person 1
8) Possible long term with person 2

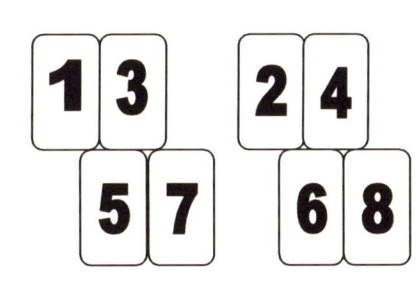

I've just met someone (dating) – We are meeting for our first date, any tips?

1) The energy/foundation of how you both met
2) Their character / personality / current focus
3) How they <u>may</u> currently feel towards you
4) What they like in a partner to heighten their emotional connection
5) What they don't like in a partner /causes them concern
6) Are they dating anyone else beside you presently
7) If you both meet up, the energy of your date with this person (place / timing)
8) If you meet, your 1st impression of them
9) If you meet, their 1st impression of you
10) Advice in order to make that 1st impression count
11) Advice in order to avoid being a turn off for them
12) What may be good about your connection together
13) What may not be so good about your connection
14) How you may feel about them after the date
15) How they may feel about you after the date
16) Likelihood of any possible future dates

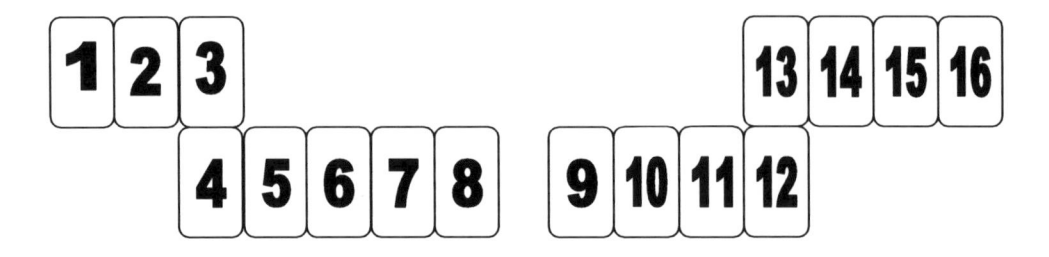

```
 1  2  3                          13 14 15 16
    4  5  6  7  8     9 10 11 12
```

I'm in two <u>intimate</u> relationships – Should I stay with <u>this one</u> or <u>that one</u>?

1) Current energy of relationship person 1
2) Current energy of relationship person 2
3) What's good about the relationship with person 1
4) What's good about the relationship with person 2
5) If you stay with person 1.....
6) If you stay with person 2.....
7) If you move on / away from both relationships....

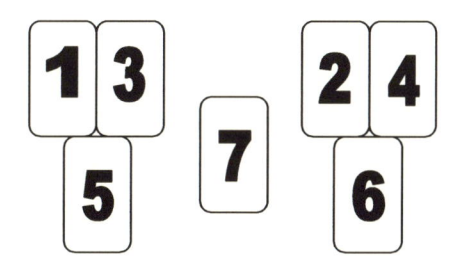

I'm kind of in a relationship – I still see my ex, but they are also seeing someone else, will they choose me over the other person? (Advanced)

1) How you currently see your relationship with your partner
2) How your partner may currently see the relationship with you
3) The relationship 'they' have with the other person
4) The type of relationship you need and desire in general
5) The type of relationship 'your partner' needs and desires in general
6) What you get from being in this 'particular' relationship
7) What your partner maybe getting from the relationship
8) What your partner maybe getting from the 'other' relationship
9) Your partner's possible feelings / thoughts on the relationship progressing short term with you
10) Your partner's possible feelings / thoughts on the relationship progressing long term with you
11) Your partner's possible feelings / thoughts on the 'other' relationship progressing short term
12) Your partner's possible feelings / thoughts on the 'other' relationship progressing long term
13) What's good about your relationship
14) What's good about 'their' relationship
15) What don't you know that could be going on in their relationship
16) If you decided to leave the relationship what's new for you
17) Advice and guidance for you, what to do now
18) Advice and guidance for you, what not to do now
19) Where your focus should be
20) Changes / developments within your relationships over the next 6 months

Please find the SPREAD layout for this on the following page

Just Real Useable TAROT SPREADS

```
        1  2  3
          4  5
        6  7  8
      9 10   11 12
       13      14
          16 15
       17 18 19 20
```

I am not sure if I'm still in a relationship – We had a massive row, I think I messed it up, have I?   (Advanced Reader)

1) The energy surrounding you both leading up to the row
2) The reason for the row/argument (Root card 1, taken from the <u>bottom</u> of the pile)
3) The part you played
4) The part they played
5) Other obstacles or factors you need to know about (unknown to you) (Root card 2)
6) The energy of the relationship now
7) How they may see or feel towards you and the relationship now
8) How you see the future relationship prospects right now
9) The possibility of them still wanting to continue / re-unite the relationship at this precise moment
10) Advice and guidance that may help to smooth things over
11) The best you can hope for over the next few weeks
12) At this moment in time... you shouldn't...
13) Where your partner (ex's) focus may be right now
14) What your focus should be on right now
15) Likelihood of a re-union on a romantic level

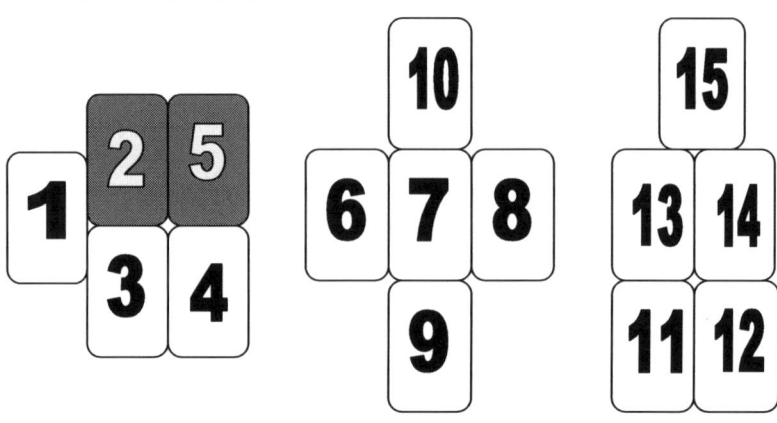

TAROT SPREADS

Work / Career / Projects / Finances

Anne-Marie Bond

I'm in work – What does the future hold?

1) The Past: How you've felt in this role
2) The Present: How you currently feel in this role
3) The Future: How you will feel in this role

I'm in work – What should I be wary of / or look forward to?

1) How you feel regarding your current role
2) The positives
3) The negatives
4) What you need to look forward to
5) What you need to be wary about
6) Changes for you over the next 6 months

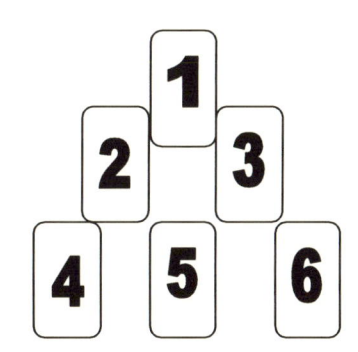

I'm in work – Should I look for another job or will things improve?

1) How you currently feel within this role
2) What is causing you to feel this way
3) Will things improve over the next few months
4) If you leave now... you can expect...
5) If you stay.... you can expect....
6) The best advice for you right now....

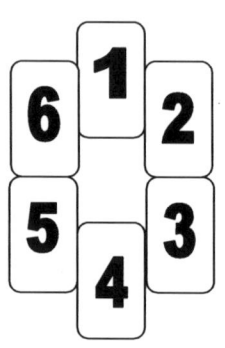

I'm in work – I've been asked to attend a meeting, will my role be affected?

1) Your current role
2) The energy of the meeting
3) Advice and guidance before attending the meeting
4) How you may feel after the meeting
5) Outcome result for your role after the meeting

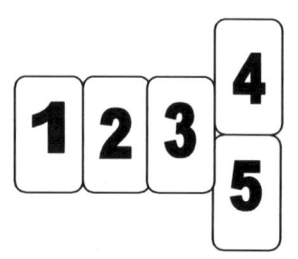

I am self-employed – How does my 'mobile' business look over the next 6 months?

1) The current energy of your *(type of business)* business
2) What you could be doing without <u>knowing</u> to hinder it's progress
3) What you are doing that's right to ensure the success of your business
4) Who / What can help you improve it
5) What action should you now take to ensure the longevity success of your business
6) How your business looks financially over the next 6 months

1 6   2 3 4 5

I am self-employed – What should I know about my business partner?

1) The current energy of your *(type of business)* business
2) How you feel towards the business
3) How my partner may feel in regards to the business
4) Obstacles or changes due to arise over the next few months (if any)
5) How we work together (good / bad)
6) How the business develops over the next year

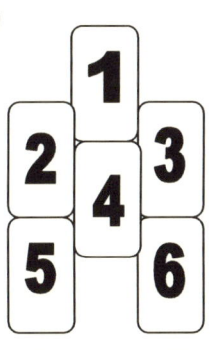

I am self-employed – Why is my business failing?

1) The current energy of your *(type of business)* business
2) What's good about it
3) The block(s) behind the scenes you may know about
4) The block(s) behind the scenes you may not know about
5) Who or what can help your business progress
6) Changes you should implement immediately
7) The status of your business in 6 months if the changes are implemented

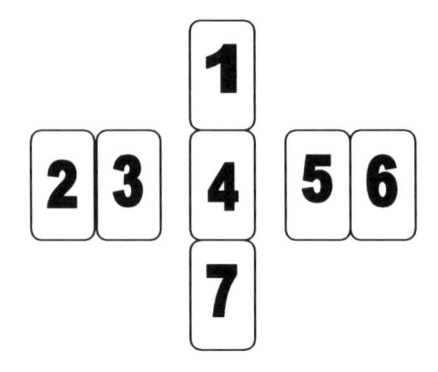

I am going to become self-employed – Will my 'new' business become successful?

1) The current energy of your *(type of business)* business
2) What's good about it / the foundation
3) What's not so good about it / area needing action
4) What could be better if you.......
5) Where your focus should be
6) The best way for you to attract more business / trade / clients / customers
7) What you need to sort out from now to avoid 'dramas' later on
8) Good stuff that you don't even know about coming up for you
9) How your business looks within its first month
10) How your business looks within its first 3 months
11) How your business looks within its first 6 months
12) How your business looks within the first 12 months
13) How your business looks within the first 24 months

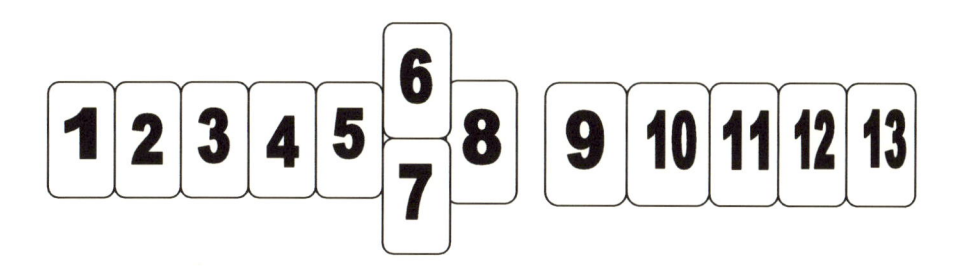

I have my own business/company – What can I do to gain more customers?

1) The current energy of your *(type of business)* business
2) The positives
3) The negatives
4) What changes you should implement to attract more customers
5) If you do follow this advice, how your business may look within 12 months
6) If you don't follow the advice, how your business may look within 12 months

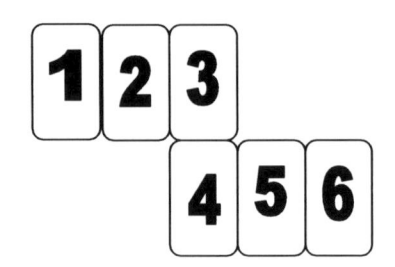

I have my own business / company – The good, the bad, the unexpected?

1) The current energy of your *(type of business)* business
2) The good points
3) The bad points
4) The unexpected - over the next 4 weeks/months expect……

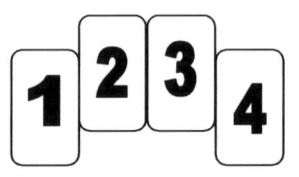

I am not working – Will I find a job soon?

1) Your current situation
2) Why you haven't found work as yet
3) Advice and guidance to help you find a job
4) If you follow the advice....
5) If you don't follow the advice....
6) Will you find a job soon?

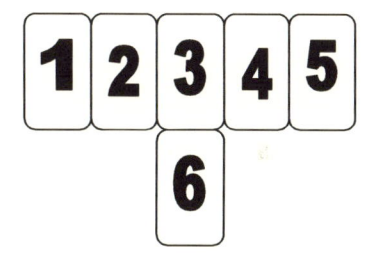

New Job – I have an interview coming up, any hints or tips?

1) Your current situation
2) You should be focusing on
3) The energy of the interview
4) How you should be / act
5) How you shouldn't be / act
6) The energy of the interviewer(s)
7) How you will feel after the interview
8) Likelihood of the interview resulting in a success for you

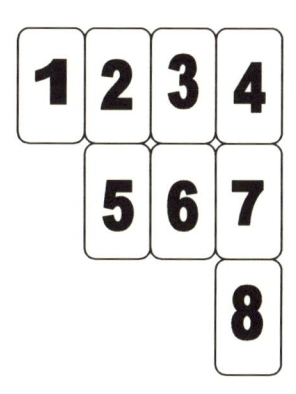

I am working on my new business *(project name)* project – Will I complete it and will it be successful?

1) The energy of your *(project name)* project / your emotional attachment to it
2) Your mental attitude towards your project
3) The effort, attitude and action you need to apply to it
4) Outside influences affecting your projects progress
5) Your optimism / hopes or projection of seeing it completed right now
6) Who / What could help you with your project
7) Don't' allow this situation/person/influence to affect you or your project
8) What other areas of your life need your focus as well
9) Cards advice in helping your project reach its final completion stage
10) How successful is the project likely to be once it's completed within the first 3 months
11) How your project may impact others or your life after the first 3 months stage
12) How does you new business project look / grow 12 months from now
13) In 1 year, are you still building upon this project or are there others you are focusing on

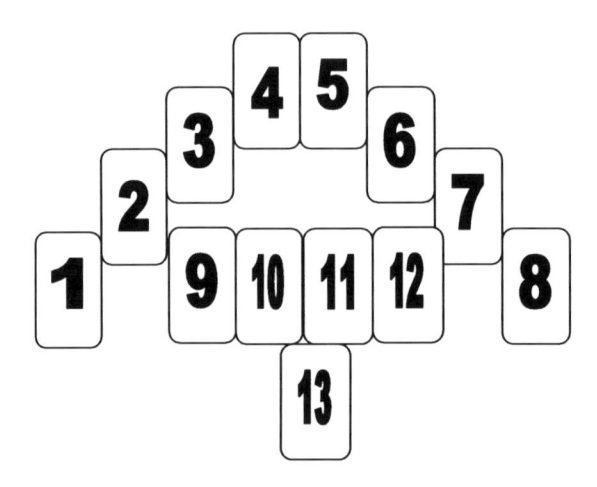

My finances – Are dire, why and will they improve?

1) **The Past:** How you've handled your finances in the past
2) Emphasis card (good / bad)
3) **The Present:** How you currently handle your finances
4) Emphasis card (good / bad)
5) **The Future:** How your finances may improve over the next few months
6) Emphasis card (good / bad)
7) How you may feel about your financial situation a year from now

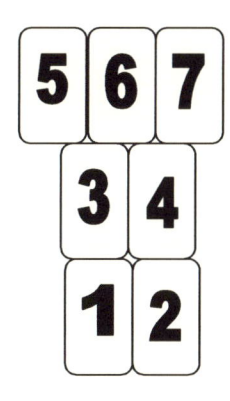

My finances – Will my idea, business plan, be financially successful?

1) The energy of your *name*/idea/ business plan
2) The foundation of it
3) The rocky part of it
4) What is <u>unknown</u> to you about it
5) Who / What may help you progress forward with it
6) Work still to be done
7) What your strengths are
8) What your weaknesses are
9) If you continue forward and stick with your plan until it's completion stage, how it looks financially at the end of its first year of launching

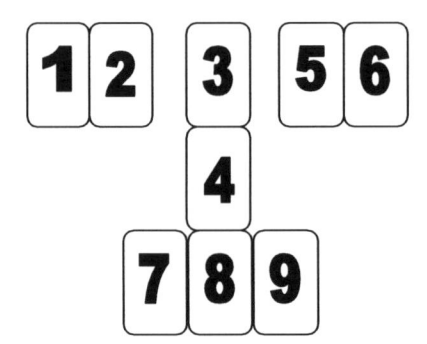

```
1 2   3   5 6
      4
      7 8 9
```

My finances – Will I be mega rich?

1) Your current financial status
2) What you need to do in order to help you become mega rich
3) Your state of mind regarding finances
4) Where your focus should be
5) Why you are not already mega rich
6) Your control with money
7) The realistic likelihood of you becoming mega rich
8) The likelihood of you becoming financially stable/comfortable

My finances – I lent some money out, will I get it back?

1) Your concerns regarding your current finances
2) Your concerns regarding the person you lent the money too
3) Their intentions of paying your money back
4) Possibility of you receiving your money
5) Your relationship with this person in the future

My finances – The good, the bad, the unexpected

1) Current energy of your finances
2) The good points
3) The bad points
4) The unexpected - over the next 4weeks/months expect......

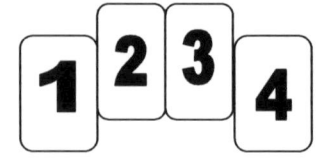

My finances – The reason why I'm broke and struggling financially

1) The way you make money
2) How you handle money
3) Your views on money
4) Why you are in your current situation financially
5) What you could change about yourself in order to attract / switch the financial energy around you
6) Then Focus on this <u>area</u> to increase your income
7) Likelihood of financial improvements over the next 3 months
8) Likelihood of financial improvements over the next 3-6 months
9) Likelihood of financial improvements over the next 6-12 months

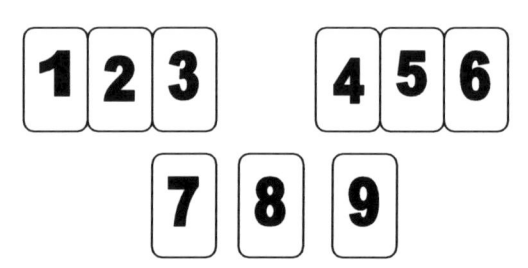

TAROT SPREADS
General Miscellaneous

My yesterday's, my today's and my tomorrow's

1) Your life in general and how it's been over the last few months to a year
2) What's been horrible – but what's been in your favour
3) What's been brilliant
4) Your current situations
5) What's good about your life right now
6) What could be better
7) Your life in general over the next year
8) Surprises in store (to embrace or for the recipient to brace themselves for)

Please note: If card 7 appears to be negative i.e. 5 coins, 3 swords etc only after placing card 8, it's ok to cap card 7 with an emphasis card to see the improvements.

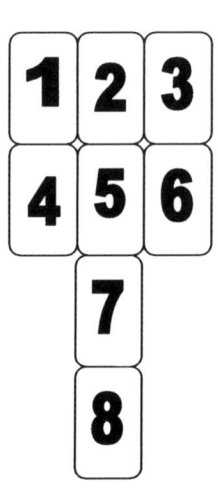

Generally, covering all areas, what does the next 3-6 months look like for me?

1) Love in general
2) Friendships in general
3) Home-life in general
4) Work or Projects in general
5) Finances in general
6) Mentally in general
7) Physically in general
8) Emotionally in general
9) Spiritually in general

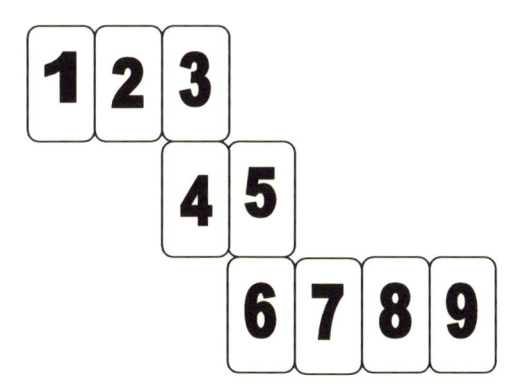

I'm thinking of starting/continuing my diet plan, will I lose weight?

1) Your current mental attitude towards your weight
2) How it affects you physically
3) How it affects you emotionally
4) How it affects you spiritually
5) Your previous weight loss attempts
6) What / Who can help you achieve their weight loss
7) How much weight should you lose in order to be happy
8) How others view your weight
9) If you were to lose your desired weight, how would you feel
10) The likelihood of losing your actual 'desired amount'
11) The likelihood of losing the 'amount' you should for health/medical reasons
12) Is the diet plan you have in mind or currently on, the right one to help you

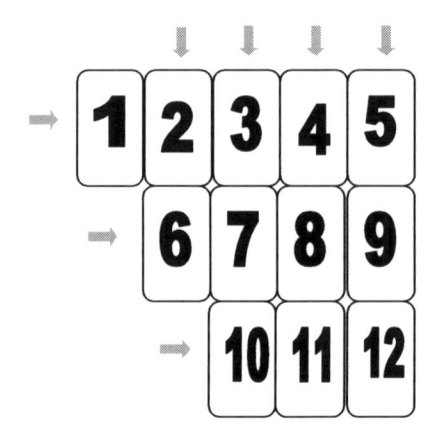

Read cards 1-12 systematically and then, downwards... 2-6, 3-10, 4-11, 5-12 for the future progression

I will be travelling soon, the good, the bad and the unexpected

1) The current energy around your trip / what your hoping for out of it
2) The good aspect part of it – whilst your there
3) The bad aspect part of it *(if any)* – whilst your there
4) What you should know about it (surprises or unexpected events)
5) How you will feel about your trip upon arriving home

What are my biggest obstacles right now, known and <u>unknown</u> to me?

1) Your biggest obstacle
2) Your biggest challenge
3) How best to overcome them both
4) Likelihood of overcoming both of them within the next year

How can I achieve a higher spiritual awareness?

1) Your current spiritual awareness / development
2) How far you could possibly develop it
3) How far you will possibly take it over the next few months
4) How the spirit world see your development
5) The personality / character of your spiritual helper
6) What will make you connect with them more on a deeper level
7) How 'other people' will be connected with your development
8) Spiritual guides helping you unknown to you (personality, description)
9) Your spiritual being before this physical world (personality, description)
10) Your spiritual awareness / development a year from now

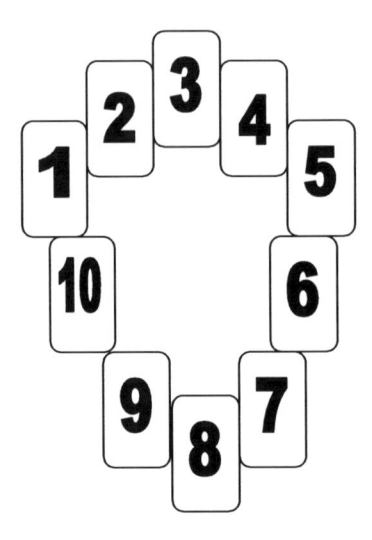

I'm told I'm psychic – am I and should I develop it?

1) How psychic are you
2) What your strengths are
3) What your weaknesses are
4) Who / What can help you develop it
5) How far could you take your development
6) What are you not doing enough of (needs to increase slightly)
7) What are you doing too much of (needs to decrease slightly)
8) If you follow your natural gut instincts, this area of your life can improve better than it is
9) Is now the right time to develop your psychic abilities
10) If and when the time is right, what would be better for you? To join a circle, a psychic centre (workshops/courses) or at home on your own using books to begin with.

(Possible answers for No 10, suggestions only, not definite answers)

Circle: 3 cups, Hierophant or cards with 3 people on it.
Psychic centre: Judgement or cards with 4 or more people in it, 10 coins.
On your own: Hermit, High Priestess, Magician, Empress, any major card with one person on it.

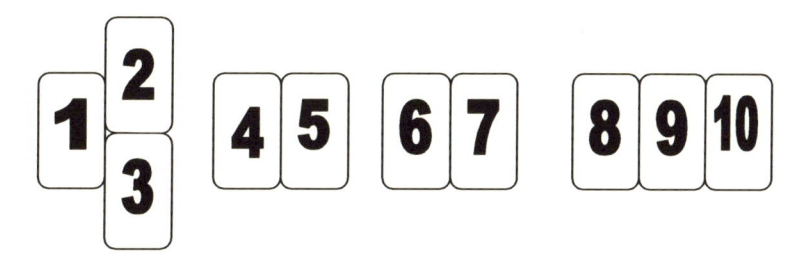

What is the best option for me – this choice or that choice?

1) Your current situation
2) Choice 1 presents....an outcome...
3) Choice 2 presents....an outcome...
4) Advice and guidance

I've been picked to go on a dinner / date / cooking / TV show, any tips?

1) Your thoughts / feelings regarding this situation
2) How you feel about it
3) The good part of it
4) The bad part of it
5) How to prepare your-self
6) What do you gain from it
7) The outcome after the event

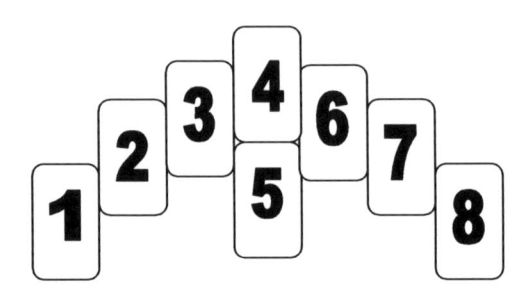

Our department is going for a re-shuffle, will I be affected?

1) Your current work situation
2) Changes to take place that may affect you
3) Changes to take place that may not affect you
4) The energy surrounding those making the 'big' decisions
5) The likely outcome for you and your role

I've got an idea to write a book, script, play would it be successful?

1) Your current thoughts / feelings towards your book/script or play idea
2) How best to proceed
3) The strengths surrounding this idea
4) What possible changes may need to take place in order for it to be published
5) At this stage the likelihood of it being started, amended and completed
6) If completed, how will others perceive it
7) If you complete it, likelihood of it being published and achieving an income from it

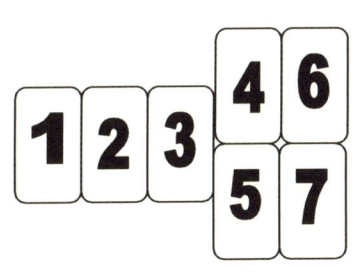

My friend is going through a hard time, what can I do to help?

1) Your friend's current situation
2) Support you could give
3) Support you shouldn't give
4) Would your friend appreciate your support
5) If you do offer your support, will it actually help their situation

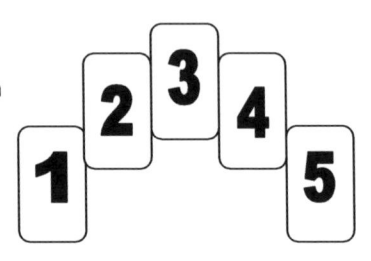

All about me: Me, Myself and I

1) Your current situation, what's going on
2) What's great about you as a person
3) What's not so great about you
4) How others see/view you
5) How you see/view yourself
6) How you affect other people
7) The positive coming up for you in a period of 7, 7days/weeks or months
8) The direction your life is heading

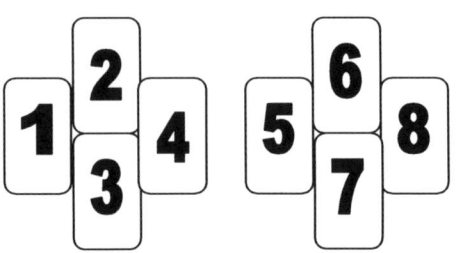

In the future, will I achieve my main desire, my dream, and my goals?

1) Your thoughts / feelings regarding you main desire
2) Obstacle in the way to hinder it materialising
3) Best advice to overcome the obstacles
4) How you are helping yourself to achieve your goals
5) Likelihood of achieving it within the year

Sometimes I feel lost, isolated, depressed and that my life is going no-where

1) Your current general situation / life focus
2) Why you have felt lost, isolated, depressed in the past, still affecting you today
3) Your mentality on life and your present circumstances
4) How you feel about others
5) How others see, view you and your situation
6) How you could help your situation to improve
7) What part you play in keeping your life as it is
8) What changes you could make in order to see significant positive life changes
9) What will happen eventually to make you feel personally fulfilled from life
10) Who or what could help you at this moment in time
11) Likelihood of you taking the advice of the cards today, tomorrow
12) Positive changes in this area for you over the next few weeks/months
13) How your life looks 6 – 12 months from now

Yes, No, Maybe (Single question answers)

1) The energy behind your question (recipient asks question aloud)
2) Where should your focus be and may still need be aware of yet to come
3) Yes, No, Maybe (the answer)

```
┌───┬───┬───┐
│ 1 │ 2 │ 3 │
└───┴───┴───┘
```

Yes: a positive card **No:** a negative card
Maybe: a middle of the road card, it's still undecided

MY SAMPLES OF YES, NO and MAYBE CARDS

In my opinion the following cards are what I use as an indication for a Yes, No or Maybe answer. Please feel free to use them in the same order, or gain your own feelings which card represents a yes, no or maybe. These are suggestions only.

Examples of a yes card:	Examples of a no card:	Examples of a maybe card:
the sun, the star, the world	death, tower, the moon	strength, hanged man, justice
ace cups, 2 cups, 3cups,	3swords, 5swords, 7swords	4cups, 6cups, 7cups, 2swords
9cups, 10cups, ace wands	10swords 4coins, 5coins, 8cups	4swords, 8coins, 5wands,
4wands, 6wands, 7wands		
ace coins, 3 coins, 7coins,		
10coins		

12 months future possibilities reading

1. Month 1
2. Month 2
3. Month 3
4. Month 4
5. Month 5
6. Month 6
7. Month 7
8. Month 8
9. Month 9
10. Month 10
11. Month 11
12. Month 12

13. **ROOT 1:** What you won't expect
14. **ROOT 2:** What you should expect

Root cards are taken from the bottom of the pack!

Readers Tip: How many major cards? Could represent the number of major changes happening over that (number) of months to come.

Anne-Marie Bond

TAROT SPREADS

Bonus: Anne-Marie's General Reading – For Advanced Readers

25 mins - Specific spread for any area (Advanced)
Before conducting this spread, choose an AREA... love...work... finances etc

Cards 8, 9 and 14 should be placed 'faced downwards'

1) Your current situation / your personality /character / focus
2) How you portray yourself to others
   & what your current problem is in relation to the area chosen

3) How others really see you
   & what your mental state is right now & what you want more of

4) Your most inner desire / hopes right now
5) Your main focus should be
6) The obstacles you're currently facing <u>known</u> to you
7) The obstacles you're facing <u>unknown</u> to you

Clients Question

8) Flavour of the Answer to the 'question' **about** to be asked (turn card 8 over)
   The recipient should now <u>ask a question</u> relating to the area chosen.
   Read the answer for this card when reading card number 9 <u>together</u>

9) Real answer (YES, NO....MAYBE)

10) 3 weeks / 3 months from now (in relation to the question or the area)
11) **ROOT 1** (taken from bottom of the deck): ....This is now the end of...
12) **ROOT 2:** (taken from bottom of the deck): ....This is now the beginning of.....
13) One year from now, what's new in your life..... and ..... (emphasis card14)

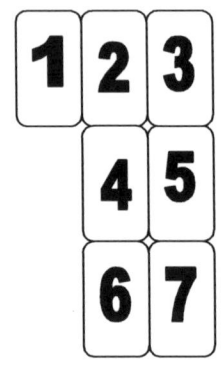

TAROT READER: To summarize the reading please read the cards randomly using a free-flow style

20 mins - Past Life Spread – who was I? (Advanced)

You will need **TWO** of the same pack, complete Pack 1's layout first, then do Pack 2 and compare.

Pack 1

1) Your current situation / personality / character TODAY
2) Problems / obstacles you are currently facing
3) Your inner desires / hopes
4) Mistakes you are currently making
5) Your strengths
6) Your weaknesses
7) The type of person others see you as
8) The type of person you'd like to be
9) Your current lifestyle
10) People who are important to you

Pack 2

1) Who you were in a previous life / character / personality
2) The problems / obstacles you faced
3) Your inner desires / hopes
4) Mistakes you made in that life time
5) Your strengths
6) Your weaknesses
7) The type of person others saw you as
8) The type of person you wanted to be
9) The lifestyle you had 'then'
10) People who were important to you then

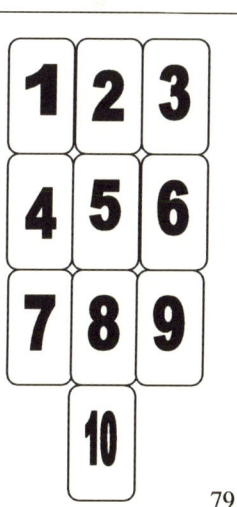

20 mins - Future Life Spread – who will I be? (Advanced)

You will need **TWO** of the same pack, complete Pack 1's layout first, then do Pack 2 and compare.

Pack 1

1) Your current situation / personality / character TODAY
2) Problems / obstacles you are currently facing
3) Your inner desires / hopes
4) Mistakes you are currently making
5) Your strengths
6) Your weaknesses
7) The type of person others see you as
8) The type of person you'd like to be
9) Your current lifestyle
10) People who are important to you

Pack 2

1) Who you are in a future life / character / personality / sex
2) Problems / obstacles you may face
3) Your inner desires / hopes
4) Mistakes you could make in that time
5) Your strengths
6) Your weaknesses
7) The type of person others see you as
8) The type of person you inspire to be
9) The lifestyle you have
10) People who are important to you

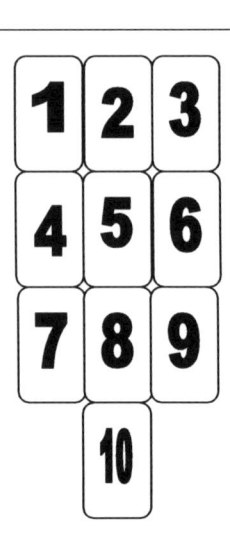

Just Real Useable TAROT SPREADS

45 mins - Future Life Progression within the next 5 years   (Advanced)

1) Your current situation / personality / character TODAY
2) Problems / obstacles you are currently facing
3) Your inner desires / hopes
4) Mistakes you are currently making
5) Your strengths
6) Your weaknesses
7) The type of person others see you as
8) The type of person you'd like to be
9) The lifestyle you have now
10) What you may achieve over the next year
11) The type of person you become In 5 years time
12) What's good for you at that time
13) What's not so good for you at that time
14) If you make better choices from today how your life may improve
15) How work or personal projects may look like for you in 5 years
16) How love or friendships or family life may look like for you in 5 years
17) What your finances may look like in 5 years
18) What looks to be your biggest achievement in 5 years
19) Your mental and emotional state 5 years from now
20) What new goals will you be setting for yourself in 5 years
21) What action can you now take in order to ensure the area you wish to improve upon the most has shown significant changes for the better in 5 years time.

TAROT READER: Summarize the major cards as the changes / developments / improvements for the recipients over the next 5 years. Using the cards on the table now answer the recipients questions.

Future Life Progression was founded by the wonderful Anne Jirsch. I have been personally taught by Anne and have been qualified and certified as Future Life Progression and Past Life Regression Therapist. I have created a Future Life Progression tarot spread in order to help those evolve spiritually, mentally, emotionally and even on a physical level, by making better choices today, helps you to live better tomorrow.

Anne-Marie Bond

TAROT SPREADS

Sample Spreads

The following spreads are based upon real readings I've conducted providing you with a snippet and brief outlook on how some of my spreads can be interpreted. Have fun with yours!

Anne-Marie Bond

Just Real Useable TAROT SPREADS

My yesterday's, my today's and my tomorrow's

1) Your life in general and how it's been over the last few months to a year
2) What's been horrible – but what's been in your favour
3) What's been brilliant
4) Your current situations
5) What's good about your life right now
6) What could be better
7) Your life in general over the next year
8) Surprises in store (to embrace or for the recipient to brace themselves for)

---

1) **7 coins**: It's been hard work for you over the last few months, you've met many challenges and at times you have been so exhausted and wondered if you would ever meet your goals. You have been planting the seeds of what you would like to accomplish over the next few months

2) **Magician**: Meeting charmers, tricksters, and especially someone who was an illusionist. You have the capability to do anything you want. You may have had problems funding your projects in the past, but you do have the skill just keep working at it and now is perhaps not the time to give up.

3) **8 coins**: Working on your hobby, what you love. Having more focus on your work and its direction.

4) **The High priestess**: Developing your spirituality and following your gut instincts. The current situation appears that you are learning and evolving onto a much higher spiritual level.

5) **Queen coins**: Making your own destiny, building your empire, being the boss and making plans for the future. Organizing what needs to be done and getting the wheels in motion.

6) **4 swords**: Getting more rest, relaxing more and finding the time to re-evaluate your focus/goals. Perhaps a new plan of action is required but at the same time do find time to recharge your batteries.

7) **3 coins**: Making headway, making progress, expanding and developing your business. Passing an exam within in 3 months seems likely and also spending money on a home or work premises to redecorate. Putting your talents on show and having other people view /assess your hard work. A very promising card.

8) **10 coins**: Money, success, business growth, family get-togethers, financially support to and from the family. Rise in income. A very promising card as it shows from the 3coins it means your hard work DOES pay off eventually and expect that over the next 10months to see a steady increase. What you have sown in the past (7coins) is about to be grow and you shall be rewarded. Having the talents and the skill to achieve it (magician) allows the possibility of it to manifest and grow into something wider than your initial expectations. Stability & permanence is also shown by this card. Success is only a few months away!

New Job – I have an interview coming up, any hints or tips?

1) Your current situation
2) What your focus should be on
3) The energy of the interview
4) How you should be
5) How you shouldn't be
6) The energy of the interviewer(s)
7) How you will feel after the interview
8) Likelihood of getting that job

---

1) **3 cups:** Right now you are happy at having this type of interview; it appears that this is a role you'd really like to get. Perhaps you are thinking also about going for a drink with friends to celebrate if the news is good.

2) **7 wands:** Standing up for yourself, fighting for what you believe in and standing your ground. Don't be a push over and don't allow others to bully you or push you into a corner. You need to stand on your own two feet now. Perhaps saying No, a bit more would be useful to you.

3) **9 swords:** Seems that you will be asked a couple of questions you may not know or wish to answer. You will be nervous before going in and wondering what they will ask of you.

4) **Ace swords:** Be direct, honest and speak up, be clear and concise with your communication.

5) **The Devil:** Give an impression of anger issues, or come across as controlling or even frustrated.

6) **Queen Swords:** A very strong minded female who knows who she is looking for to complete this role. She will stand no-nonsense and will appreciate your truth and honesty when answering her questions

7) **Hanged man:** In limbo, almost as if you were expecting to know if you got the job there and then, but having to be told there is a wait before knowing the result. You will also try to see if perhaps you could have answered the questions in a different way. Don't beat yourself up and just be patient.

8) **2 cups:** A great connection therefore a good result is likely. The interviewer will hire the one that they feel most suitable to the role. With this card it shows that the possibility of getting that role seems really strong in your corner and you never know perhaps making a friend for life in the process.

I am self-employed – How does my business look over the next 6 months?

1) The current energy of your *(type of business)* **business**
2) What you're doing to hinder it's progress
3) Who / What can help you improve it
4) What you are doing right
5) How your business looks over the next 6 months

```
  1        2
      3
  5        4
```

1) **7 coins:** It appears to be hard work at present, a lot of effort and hard work has been invested, but you are probably not so happy with the pace as you want to see the results sooner than later.

2) **9 cups:** Thinking that everything is bright and breezy, or perhaps putting on a good face that everything is ok. Don't be too contented or get to complacent as this could really hinder you.

3) **3 swords:** No-one, this is about you getting over the hurt people having caused you in the past. It could also be the time to perhaps think about separating from it a little bit. Ignore the rejection you've received from others and don't let past hurt affect you at this time in your life. It's time to dust yourself off stand up straight and just get on with things and don't worry about feeling vulnerable this is just the process you have to go through. Clearer communication of what you want also helps.

4) **2 coins:** Taking things easy, juggling and balancing all aspects of it. Working on small projects along side to help bring the money element back into balance. So far what you're doing right is by keeping the cost of the business at the right price. You are coping really well with all the different demands daily life presents you. By being flexible you are allowing the smooth running of your business to unfold and starting the wheels in motion through electronic media's, getting yourself heard also.

5) **Page cups:** Something new that hasn't even been thought about as yet could be created from this business. It's almost like from out of nowhere a new avenue is offered. Teaching is indicated also over the next 6 months and you could be invited to discuss your business plans or ideas with a much wider audience and possibly more influential people. Your creativity is what will really spring board your business onto new heights and levels. Time to get creating.

All about me: Me, Myself and I

1) Your current situation, what's going on
2) What's great about you as a person
3) What's not so great about you
4) How others see/view you
5) How you see/view myself
6) How you affect other people
7) What's positive coming up for you in a period of 7, 7days, weeks or months?
8) Today you need to know that:....

---

1) **The Star:** You are sending your wishes up and are asking the universes for help. You appear to be thinking about changing your image somehow, and perhaps even thinking about changing your hair style. The star card is great as it shows your focus is set and you can almost see what is truly possible. Hope is restored.

2) **The Devil:** You are strong, you are impulsive and spontaneous. You know how to heal others and stop an argument or tension brewing. You have firm control of what you want (the star) and with the devil you have no intention of giving it up. Your confidence is growing rapidly.

3) **9 swords:** You are a born worrier, you stress too much and you live with guilt and regret. As much as having the strength of the devil, sometimes you wonder if you come on too strong. You are a loner and you don't like to show your feelings especially when you feel vulnerable or lonely. You tend to deal with problems on your own and you do have a tendency to over analyze situations that aren't really as bad as you make out.

4) **4 wands:** Others see you as a strong, stable and secure person. Your world looks fun and inviting, because of this you may find others naturally gravitate to you. People will love be in your home and feel protected there.

5) **The chariot:** You see yourself as a person who's in control of their own destiny. Any victory you achieve is usually down to your own hard work and not because it fell into your lap. You have learnt to control your emotions / bad habits somewhat which now help to direct you on to the right path.

6) **King cups:** You affect others through your calmness and your guidance, teaching or counsel. You are very creative and kind and generous. You are thoughtful, independent & perhaps fail to get as much exercise as you should. You help other people by indentifying their needs & providing tangible solutions.

7) **3 cups:** Celebrations, congratulations, out with friends celebrating. A birthday party in 3 weeks to look forward to. This says that you will have a great time with friends and celebrate something you have achieved, been recognized or rewarded for!

8) **6 cups:** You need to know that someone from your past is making a return, expect to see a blast from the past within 6 weeks. It also appears that you receive a gift or kind gesture when you least expect it. Discussion of children also, but more about setting up or achieving new heights in a business. This is a trade card & suggests that your business with the (3cups) will begin to flourish especially within a period of 9 weeks.

Yes, No, Maybe (Single question answers)

Recipient to say their question aloud, before shuffling!

1) The energy of the question in mind
2) Why is the recipient asking this question
3) Yes, No, Maybe (the answer)

Question:
Will I be in a romantic & committed relationship within the next 3 months?

1) **3 cups:** This is something you really want. There could be a possibility of a romance with a close friend if you wanted it, but right now you seem to be quite happy with your mutual friendships. However you are wanting someone you can be friends with first and then perhaps even lead to marriage eventually.
2) **6 cups:** Because you are thinking about someone from your past. You are still holding onto the memory of someone else and perhaps now wishing to erase that memory by connecting with someone new. It could also represent that you want children or that you feel like a child and need someone to help you or if reversed maybe you need someone to show you how to have fun again.
3) **8 wands:** This is an unexpected affair card. So it suggests that over the next 8 weeks you may have a quick and speedy romance and may come from the last place (or person) you'd think. This simply means where your love life has been stagnant it appears with this card that your romance area is now looking up and someone is on the cards and will be brought to you on a speed boat (metaphorically speaking). There is also an indication of receiving a call from an ex within the next 8 days / weeks.

I'm single – Why can't I meet anyone compatible and will I someday?

1) Your mental / emotional state
2) Your past relationships
3) The positives you bring into a relationship
4) The type of person that would be compatible to you
5) What hinders you currently attracting a decent partner
6) What / Who could help you find someone compatible
7) All about the type of person I probably will meet next
8) Possible timings / and how or where the meeting takes place
9) <u>Generally:</u> what's coming up for you soon

An email reading:

1) **The World:** You are thinking about business expansion, spreading your wings. It appears that you could also be trying to complete a project or see something through to its completion stages. Perhaps you are also thinking about travel or connecting with people from different parts of the country or world

2) **Knight of Swords:** This energy tells me you were involved with an air sign. Someone quite strong minded (or willed), a very hard person to persuade otherwise once their mind is made up. This person may have had a tendency to be aggressive or perhaps appeared that way to others. A strong person, intelligent, quick thinking and will rush to the defence of others. They definitely know how to protect themselves. They are good at getting out of trouble due to their quick thinking ways and perhaps at times could be quite cold with their communication or maybe appeared distant at times. Don't' expect too many compliments from this type of character as they can be quite selfish.

3) **8 cups:** The positives of what you brought into the relationship was to 'stay' longer involved than what you should have done. When you should have walked away you didn't because you were emotionally attached and maybe wanted to make things work. Eventually you plucked the courage to walk away.

4) **King Wands:** A fire sign (Aries, Leo, Sagittarius) whose character is warm, loving, passionate. A strong individual, business minded, an entrepreneur, focused, driven, stable, protective, family oriented, loyal, a provider, a leader and someone who isn't frightened over carrying the reigns.

5) **King cups:** Another man, or yourself as you are a Cancerian. It possible means you are sitting on your bum for too long and not going out there to meet people. Perhaps you're waiting for Mr Right, to come to you? You need to be more flexible and start showing a side of relaxation, calmness and openness to you.

6) **Ace of swords:** This isn't about someone else, this is about you. Find your voice, speak up. Be clear and precise in what you are looking for, don't' give mixed signals. It's about a new way of thinking, and being prepared to speak the truth, by saying how you feel and what it is you're after. Become more dynamic with your conversation and show your 'intelligence' because you really are. You are the key to success here but you've just got to break through the 'bad seed' of people you have been attracted to in the past, and now go for the more intelligent, witty and serious type of people. Those that tell you exactly how it is, how they feel about you and themselves, clear in their communication also. No jibber, jabber, straight to the point.

Accept new invitations as they arrive as you are bound to receive an invitation to go somewhere within the next week or month... Go for it, even if it seems not a good idea at first, it will probably be the last place you expect to meet someone..... and then....???

7) **Knight of wands:** This person is still on their road to be the king of wands (which we saw earlier) that would be the person you'd be most compatible with.

They have ideas about their direction and where they are heading in life, both for work and relationships. This person will travel with their work and maybe located in a different area to where you live or work. They are passionate, considerate, albeit a bit challenging at times and at the best of times even slightly cocky. This person is very sincere, sure of themselves, outgoing, likes being outdoors and knows where they are heading in life.

Sometimes though they can project an unrealistic image or target for themselves. They are not shy in coming forward and blowing their own trumpet. Their other side, is the shy and reserved side, the quite side and even withdrawn at times, and this is apparent if they are unsure of how you feel about them, they would rather you confess your feelings first before they do. This person has a strong work ethic but also has strong family ties and connections.. Once things develop between you both they will want to stabilize a firmer foundation with you and may try to pull out all the stops to secure you as belonging to them. They will do their best to keep you, provide for you and protect you.

8) **King of swords:** Winter time December to February and possibly through a male friend

9) **Ace of wands:** New beginnings both in business/personal projects and love and the fact the Ace represents a number one, also indicates that January donates a great and positive month for both these areas as being significant changes for the better in your life!

Anne-Marie Bond

Just Real Useable TAROT SPREADS

MY SERVICES

Psychic Readings — *Private 1-2-1 or email psychic, tarot readings*

Spiritual Readings — *Private 1-2-1 mediumship readings*

FLP — *Future Life Progression, find out your future over the next 5 -10 years. Meet your future self and gain valuable advice in order to achieve a better-life style*

PLR — *Past Life Regression, find out who you were before being born into this lifetime, what are the traits you still carry?*

FLT — *Future Lifetime, find out whom you will be after departing this lifetime, will you meet up with anyone you now know?*

WEIGHT-LOSS — *Should you wish to lose weight, I am an independent Cambridge weight plan consultant and see clients wanting to solely attend my weight-loss programme. Having lost over* **9 stone** *myself on my programme and combing my FLP session it works!* **Call: (UK) 07950 612 422** annesweightplan@gmail.com

MY WORKSHOPS - Teaching

I run various workshops and private 1-2-1 sessions for beginners, intermediate and advanced level students covering psychic and spiritual development. Please contact me if you would like to book yourself in for any of the courses I have on offer or for a private reading with me.

- ✓ **Tarot Reading** — *learn how to interpret the cards for yourself or others*
- ✓ **Tarot Master-class** — *become a professional online / telephone psychic reader*
- ✓ **Tarot Spreads** — *learn how to create your own tarot spreads...that work*
- ✓ **Psychic Development** — *learn to feel & trust your gut instincts – read for others or yourself*
- ✓ **Spiritual Development** — *mediumship - learn to connect with loved ones in the spirit world*
- ✓ **Psychic Circle - Run your own** — *how to start a circle, tips of the trade and mistakes to avoid*

CONTACT ANNE-MARIE:

My Services or General questions

Psychic, Tarot, Spiritual, Workshops, FLP

Contact: Anne-Marie Bond
Phone: 07949 897 065
Email: spiritualstars@gmail.com

Weight-Loss: 07950 612 422
               annesweightplan@gmail.com

www.tarotreading4u.co.uk   www.spiritualstars.webs.com   www.fastdietweightloss.webs.com

Just Real Useable TAROT SPREADS

4173450R00055

Printed in Great Britain
by Amazon.co.uk, Ltd.,
Marston Gate.